THE MONEY TO CONTROL

HOW THE ELITE CONSPIRE AGAINST YOU

DECONSTRUCTING AMERICA PART 2

TOM S. PANE

FOREWORD

THIS book is the second part of a series entitled *Deconstructing America*, which attempts to explain, in a relatively easy-to-understand way, how the ultra-rich use their vast power and resources to manipulate the general population into supporting their beliefs and interests. The series will look at different aspects of how power is used to control people, all within the framework of the founding and development of the United States of America, to illustrate its arguments and support its conclusions.

The first book in the series, *The Power to Control*, talks about how control is applied against the population by those in power through a variety of methods which include: the retelling of historical events in a narrative that aligns to the goals of the rich; the use of propaganda and the institutional framework of laws, courts and police to repress the majority in support of the wealthy elite minority; and an interconnected system of indoctrination programming and ongoing conditioning intended to help reinforce all of the above. The first book also discussed how elites use words and language, as well as the illusion of choice, to give American citizens the impression they live in a just and fair society.

While reading the first book is not required to understand this one, I would recommend you read it first (it only takes an hour or two) to set the stage for this discussion. *The Money to Control* will primarily focus on how elites use economics and their control over industries and capital investment to conspire against average citizens, transferring wealth from working- and middle-class pockets into the bank accounts of the ultra-rich.

This book, like *The Power to Control*, will use Howard Zinn's *A People's History of the United States* as a foundation for facts and data to support the historical elements of this pamphlet's narrative. A primary concept of the whole series is to present ideas typically found in more academic books like Zinn's, but in a much easier-to-consume format that's understandable by pretty much anyone. This book, like the first, is intended to be read in a single sitting.

In *The Money to Control*, I will focus on how the ultra-rich use their own personal wealth, their influence with the government, and their ownership of industries and private property not only to repress and keep the lower classes unable to challenge their rule but to steadily bleed the lower classes dry of their wealth through overwork and exploitation. This book will also examine how the elite managed to install a shadow Corporate State under the mask of Democracy during the late 19th and early 20th century.

One of the reasons I focus on historical events in these first books, rather than present-day events, is that I feel it is critical to reset and reorient the conversation about what is happening in America by returning to the root incidents that led to the state we are in now. Until we can strip away decades of misinformation and disinformation that have obfuscated the facts about how money is used to pit one group against another, as well as weaken them to abuse and persecution by the state and the rich, no solution can be achieved, since the right conversations are simply not taking place.

We need to go back…back to the period after the Civil War as our society was being reshaped, not by the Constitution or any form of centralized social planning, but by legions of lawyers for large corporations which, along with their partners in the

Government, created and evolved a game of loaded dice which has the appearance of fairness and equality, but in actuality is geared to benefit the elite few at the expense of the many.

While *The Power to Control* examined how power is wielded to control the masses through historical precedent up to the Civil War, The Money to Control will examine events after the war, as reconstruction was ending, and the next phase of economic development and social unrest occurred in tandem. During this time, the rich benefitted from advances in technology and production, while ordinary workers saw their conditions worsen.

By the end of this reading, you should be armed with information on several core issues that must be addressed before America can set a path that is not inherently self-destructive or regressive. These issues changed how the buyer and seller relate and interact with each other, how corporations are viewed in the eyes of the law and state, and how the myth of American exceptionalism and rags-to-riches is used to manipulate the ordinary person into blindly supporting an elitist oligarchy.

The goal of this book is to allow you, the inhabitants of America, to live a freer and more authentic life by possessing alternate information that those in charge have decided not to provide to you.

IN much of the world, but especially in the United States of America, there are often double meanings in how things are presented to people, versus what they actually are. The America we all know and have been told about in school, at work, in movies, in books, and in the media is the America of democracy, freedom, justice, equality, and opportunity.

This narrative framework is meant to shape and illustrate our society to young people and the world at large, in line with the image it seeks to portray – one that is positive, self-serving, and manufactured. This promoted vision of the United States is pure fantasy, with little connection to the real world and totally unsupported by scientific data or historical precedent.

Let's use the modern corporation as an example to illustrate what the USA's actual goals and objectives are, versus what they tell the public they are. By definition, and this is not a debatable or controversial statement, for-profit companies care about one thing and one thing only – making money (revenue and profit). They want to make as much of it as possible, as fast as possible, with as few employees as possible. That is the actual corporate goal of all companies within our modern economic system. All other objectives are subservient to that one and are geared and designed to support the goal of maximizing revenue and profitability.

All companies, like the government, have public relations (PR) departments whose job is to put out propaganda to support their viewpoints and goals. Propaganda is information designed to manipulate people into taking an action or adopting a way of thinking. It, by definition, is not news or information meant to educate; quite the opposite. For corporations, that may be to tell their corporate narrative, which is a nice story to make you think that making money is not all they care about. For example, an insurance company donates nominal amounts to a kid's cancer charity. They don't donate this money because they care about kids or curing cancer, far from it. They give out the money as both a tax mitigation strategy, but mainly to improve the public's impression and image of the company. That is the goal of PR, which is just a nice modern name for propaganda.

The United States of America, which is, in essence, more like a massive conglomerate corporation than a sovereign country, has the same kind of PR a corporation has about its mission, including who founded it, how it came to be, and what its values are. America, just like corporations, has its own PR departments, both in the form of government agencies (CDC, FDA, EPA) that promote a point-of-view from whichever faction of the oligarchy (D, R) they represent at the time, but also in the form of corporate media (NYT, MSNBC, CNN, FOX), think tanks (CATO, CAP), Universities, and private businesses that work hand-in-hand with the government to spread and disseminate the image of America its owners and leaders want you to see and believe in. Just as in a for-profit company, the real America has little to do with the carefully crafted PR image developed over the past few centuries.

In this book and the *Deconstructing America* series as a whole, we will peel back the layers of the onion that is the myth of America, cleverly constructed over the past two centuries, exposing the true motivations and founding factors that have led to our current state of affairs.

CONTENTS

BY now, you know the America-approved PR version of the Civil War, how it was this grand battle of good and evil, as the noble and non-racist North fought the bigoted South to free the blacks out of the goodness of their hearts and disgust for the institution of slavery. And there was this great leader named Abraham Lincoln, who was a swell guy, and he won the war and liberated the blacks to a life of equality and personal freedom. The Civil War, as we have all been told, was a war of liberty and a war of justice.

I'm not going to spend time debating this narrative, since we will go post-war and beyond, but I address it in The Power to Control if you want my viewpoint. What the Civil War did was transfer the center of power from the South to the Northeast, where a new aristocracy was emerging that needed to solidify its rule and ownership of the national economy and the forces that served it, such as the U.S. Government.

During the Civil War, the U.S. government had a lot of leeway to do terrible things to its citizens, things it liked doing and wanted to keep doing post-war. This way, they could keep working people from complaining too much, as well as ensure the nation's new owners sitting plush in their northern mansions would not be molested by the riff-raff on their way to brunch. Oh, and by leeway, I mean how violent and repressive the government can be to keep people down and in line with what their handlers, the oligarchy, want.

For example, during the Civil War, if workers dared to go on strike for better wages, they would be violently attacked by soldiers and forced back to work at gunpoint, something that would continue for decades as government, police, and private strikebreaker goons were employed to keep workers quiet and working for starvation wages. Anyone who expressed vocal opposition to Abraham Lincoln's wartime policies was jailed without trial or due process. Upwards of 30,000 American citizens were imprisoned as political prisoners during the Civil War for sedition and dissent. The Great Emancipator indeed.

At this time, it was already apparent to the people in charge that a primary feature of the new economic system (capitalism) they were embracing was that, due to reckless speculation and profiteering, cyclical panics and depressions were completely unavoidable. What the rich figured out back then was that these economic downswings allowed them to exploit and profit from people below them who were suffering. In bad times in America, you will see time and time again that the ruling elite will exploit a terrible situation to their benefit and profit, all at the general population's expense.

For example, during the Civil War, the prices of milk, eggs, and cheese rose by 60-100%. According to historian Emerson Fite (quote is edited to modernize the language) —

"Employers were accustomed to giving themselves all or nearly all the profits accruing from the higher prices, without being willing to grant to the employees a fair share of these profits through the medium of higher wages."

Huh. Does this sound familiar in our modern times, and what has happened during the COVID pandemic? That companies jacked up prices and reduced the size of packaging, all to gouge consumers when they are hurting the most? And those same companies that are increasing profit are not raising wages and benefits when times are good, but they sure cut them quickly when times are bad. The financial strategy of the elite in the United States of America has always been to use economic hardship and national disasters as opportunities to rob and exploit the working and middle classes and transfer wealth upwards in spurts.

One way the elite exercise control over the ordinary citizen is through their outsized influence in government. Their partners in the government will pass laws that appear to benefit the everyday person, but, in reality, are designed to give free handouts to the rich under the cloak of social support. This is what they call subsidies, or did when they were a little more honest about their intentions.

SINCE the 1950s, the government has funneled money through the Pentagon to provide billions in free technology research and development (R&D) to private companies, who then monetize and profit from those inventions with no strings attached. They started doing this after WW2 as a way to hide subsidies and free cash for the rich and private companies, by moving it through the Pentagon and calling it 'defense spending'. So now subsidies are called defense, and Congress can't fall over itself fast enough to rubber-stamp their approval for their actual constituents, the ultra-rich.

Ever wonder where hundreds of billions in untraceable cash and funding that the Pentagon can't account for go each year? The Pentagon has never conducted a successful audit to determine where the money goes. Ever wonder what happened to the Star Wars defense project from the 80s? It was never made real, but billions were spent on R&D. Guess who invented the internet? The Defense Advanced Research Projects Agency (DARPA). Do you see any private companies paying us back or paying taxes on the public money that was used to provide digital infrastructure to these businesses? Who benefited and profited from all this research? American oligarchs who own companies and dominate industries are who.

Way back then, as now, the government and corporations, working hand in hand, had many ways to appear to assist the American people while funneling that money into the pockets of the rich. For example, in 1862, the Homestead Act was passed. The Act intended to give 160 acres of land out West to anyone who would cultivate it for 5 years for a payment of $200. The PR story was that it enabled the West to be populated with regular Joes. But the reality of the Act was that, back then, $200 was out of reach for anyone except the very rich, so real estate speculators and railroads took much of the land supposedly intended for ordinary citizens.

Does this sound familiar to what is happening today with the Covid PPP small business loan program, which was meant to save small businesses during the pandemic but was, in fact, taken by large, public for-profit companies and wealthy individuals due to loopholes deliberately inserted by colluding politicians? It's a trick and sleight of hand that the elite and their lackeys in the government have been doing for over a century. Make public money look like it is going to the public to help them, so they support it and don't complain, then put it in legalized language to actually divert that money into the pockets of the donor class. Rinse and repeat for decades.

IN the 30 years leading up to the Civil War, United States federal and local laws were increasingly interpreted to benefit businesses at the expense of community interests. A good example of this is the law of **eminent domain**. Let's say you are a homesteader who had the $200 for a homestead out west, and you got some land and were living somewhere a railroad needed to pass through. The railroad may have offered you a few bucks, and you refused, or just not offered anything and waited for their buddies in the government to take care of it. The government would use eminent domain (the only thing it was ever used for) to simply take a farmer's land and give it to the railroad company, for free. Oh, ok, maybe there were some kickbacks or bribes in the backroom somewhere to make it happen.

Another example of how the law was modified to be used against the ordinary citizen was when court judgments for damages against businesses were taken out of the hands of citizen juries and given to judges, who conveniently were rich appointees of the ruling class. Other changes made around this time included replacing private arbitrations (outside the court) with court settlements, which increased reliance on lawyers and the legal system to resolve cases. This gave the rich more control over the process since they were the only ones who could afford adequate legal representation. The massive legal system you see around you was created deliberately so the rich could keep you out of the legal process through financial means. You can't afford to fight them through it.

Happening since the 16th century, but taken to a new level during the mid to late 19th century, the commercial relationship between seller and buyer was transformed from long-standing ancient practices that governed such transactions. The ancient concept of a fair and honest deal for both buyer and seller led to the modern idea of caveat emptor, more commonly known as **Let the Buyer Beware**. This foundational legal concept holds that, in certain situations, defects in goods or services may be legally hidden from the buyer and known only to the seller. This shift in commercial interactions between buyer and seller from **fair price** to **watch your back** is fundamental to how the rich have been able to loot American citizens and resources, and how the modern system of predatory capitalism has flourished.

Ever watched Judge Judy? She loves to talk about buyer beware and how it is the buyer's fault for getting ripped off by a con man. Somehow, you should have known something you couldn't have known, and you have to pay for it, not the criminal party who lied to you.

"By the middle of the 19th century, the legal system had been reshaped to the advantage of men of commerce and industry at the expense of farmers, workers, consumers, and other less powerful groups within society…it actively promoted a legal redistribution of wealth against the weakest groups in the society." – Horowitz.

The whole goal here was to disguise and legitimize the law's exploitation of the weak and vulnerable, while giving it the appearance of fairness and neutrality. This has worked like a charm to keep people under control by keeping them poor and helpless in the face of institutional power.

IN 1873, the failure of a too-big-to-fail bank triggered a market panic. These panics and market crashes seemed inevitable due to a new economic and social theory that had been developing since the 16th century, called capitalism. There were periodic crashes of the U.S. economy in 1837, 1857, 1873, and later in 1893, 1907, 1919, and 1929, with each wiping out small businesses and putting people out of work while wealthy families like the Vanderbilts, Astors, Rockefellers, and Morgans made their fortunes betting on the up and down process of war and peace, crisis and recovery. The 1873 crisis led to Andrew Carnegie's monopoly in the steel market and to the Rockefellers' dominance in oil through Standard Oil.

Does this sound a bit like what happened today during the pandemic, as billionaires made billions? At the same time, the rest of us went broke, got evicted, and blamed an unfortunate situation beyond our control. To illustrate this, in 2009, Bill Gates was worth $40 billion. In 2021, after the pandemic, he was worth $154 billion. In 2009, Mark Zuckerberg was worth $2 billion. In 2021, he was worth $140 billion. Wages during this time were stagnant at best across all levels of workers.

Just as now, back then, there were angry people protesting the injustices they were suffering at the hands of the rich. Just like now, those protests and strikes were met with a violent response by the police. A newspaper at the time reported on a protest of workers, including women and children, in Tompkins Square in 1874, who were attacked by the police –

"Police clubs rose and fell. Women and children ran screaming in all directions. Many of them were trampled underfoot in the stampede for the gates. In the street, bystanders were ridden down and mercilessly clubbed by mounted officers."

By 1877, the United States of America was in a deep depression. Workers were not happy. In dozens of cities, railroad workers went on strike after their wages were cut, and federal troops were sent in, paid by bankers and oligarchs, to get the trains moving again. As things escalated, the troops were soon shooting down strikers. A rally of 6,000 people protested that they wanted to nationalize the railroads when the police attacked, as reported.

"The sounds of clubs falling on skulls was sickening for the first minute until one grew accustomed to it. A rioter dropped at every whack, it seemed, for the ground was covered with them."

Interesting to note that the press, even back then, often called protesters or strikers rioters. Dozens of unarmed and peaceful people were murdered by the police that day. Blaming the victim has a long history in the old US of A. During the Great Railroad Strike of 1877, more than 100,000 workers went on strike. As was standard policy, they were violently attacked by the government and police, with 100 people dead and 1,000 sent to jail.

To not only keep wages down but also keep workers under control and in their place, wealthy industrialists set up a social class tiering system for unskilled laborers based on criteria such as race, religion, ethnicity, and social standing. For example, women, blacks, and immigrant laborers from China were all compensated and rewarded differently based on those criteria (not skill, talent, ability, etc.). It was immigrants from Europe and China who made up much of this new, unskilled, easy-to-exploit workforce.

THERE is an assumed truth in America about how the system or country itself somehow leads to the creation of self-made men through its innovative approach to capital and individual greed. This erroneous assumption was developed through a series of entertainment and propaganda pieces from the 19th century, used to sell books and to convince people to work themselves to death for the profit of others.

A large part of the American exceptionalism fantasy is based on the Horatio Alger myth. This comes from a series of pulp fiction books from the late 1900s in which a poor man rises from **rags to riches** through his superior moral character, American exceptionalism, and the generosity of the rich. The writer Horatio Alger, like other 19th-century mainstream writers, helped shape the American mythos that we now call U.S. culture. A mixture of narrative fiction within the historical framework of the country, with idealized characters and noble goals. In all his books, there is a poor young man who does good deeds and gets noticed by a rich man, who then rewards the poor boy with a middle- or upper-class lifestyle. The boy himself fails, but because he follows society's stated values, he is rewarded by the ruling class for toeing the line.

The reality is that, back then, as now, most rich people came from wealthy backgrounds with outsized financial advantages or inherited their money.

A study of the origins of 303 textile, railroad, and steel executives from the 1870s found that 90% came from middle- to upper-class families. Today, 40% of all wealth is inherited.

So, the idea that you pull yourselves up by the bootstraps and make your own way really only applies to some of us. Those rich kids who inherited Daddy's money are the ones running our companies, running our government, and benefiting from their positions of being born to the right family, regardless of their talent, intelligence, skill, or moral character. Meritocracy indeed.

The reality is that the U.S. government, in a series of laws and sweetheart deals with corporations, has given and continues to give away massive amounts of free money (public) and land to the rich. Those corporations got cheap labor overseas, just like they do now, so they could abuse them, exploit them, and pit them against American workers, forcing wages down and increasing their profits even more. For example, the Central Pacific Railroad bribed our government to get 9 million acres of free land, while paying a construction company that they owned almost 100% more than the work actually cost. The company brought in 3,000 Irish and 10,000 Chinese workers and paid them $1-2 a day for 4 years. Workers died by the hundreds in brutal conditions while being subject to Indian attacks.

Are you starting to get it now? It has always been this way **by design** in the United States of America. The government is in bed with the elites and their corporations by giving them free money (ours), land (ours too), and other resources through bribes and kickbacks (all now legalized through legislation). The rich who own the companies then bring in overseas workers for peanuts and abuse and exploit them for even more individual profit, all while taking work away from American citizens, driving down domestic wages, and fermenting community racial tensions. All of this is to give a rich person another mega yacht, another mansion they don't live in, and another billion dollars they will never use.

Want another example of how ethical our great industrial titans who built America were?

J.P. Morgan was a banker. He used his vast resources to buy 5,000 rifles for $3.50 each during the Civil War and sold them to a General in the field for $22 each, a 529% profit margin. It turned out the rifles were defective and would shoot off the thumbs of soldiers who were using them. The sale was reviewed by Congress and determined to be valid and legal, no problem at all (Let the Buyer Beware!).

BY the late 19ᵗʰ century, bankers and industrialists (then more honestly called **robber barons**) had solidified their control over US infrastructure and resources. Then, in 1895, the United States' gold reserve was depleted. This is odd for a country experiencing such rapid industrial growth and financial success, especially given that 26 NYC banks held $129 million in gold in their vaults. J.P. Morgan and some other bankers offered to **Bail Out** the US government and give it gold in exchange for government bonds. President Grover Cleveland agreed, and the bankers immediately sold the bonds they were given for an $18 million profit. Patriots indeed.

With the US government lacking centralized planning, which instead relied on the market and businesses to determine a path forward, bankers like J.P. Morgan helped bring structure and organization to the national railroad, banking, and insurance systems.

But with so much outsized power and control, guys like J.P. Morgan also wanted to create and maintain monopolies that eliminated fair competition from the marketplace. For example, J.D. Rockefeller owned the Standard Oil Company and made secret agreements with railroads to give them oil at discounted rates, driving competitors out of business. This pattern was repeated around the country. Businessmen made millions and built empires by eliminating competition, keeping prices high and wages low, and securing government subsidies for free land and money.

By the turn of the century, monopolies were all over the country, from the telephone system to farm machinery. Banks had corporate directors on the boards of multiple companies to exert central control. For example, J.P. Morgan sat on the board of 48 corporations, and Rockefeller on 37. Their influence extended far beyond the companies they directly controlled.

All the fantastic news and profit for robber barons didn't translate into higher wages and better treatment of workers; in fact, quite the opposite. Without substantive labor laws, workers were used, abused, and exploited for their labor for very little, all at risk to their own lives, without any avenue for recourse. In 1889, 22,000 railroad workers were killed or injured on the job.

From the late 19th century onward, America became a pure capitalist state with a ruling oligarchy using the framework of a democratic state for outward appearances and conflict resolution. The United States federal and state governments pretend to be neutral between the rich and everyone else to maintain order, but they actually serve only the interests of the elite. Since the rich don't always agree with each other, someone needs to help settle their disputes. This is what the United States government's true goal and objective is. To settle upper-class disputes peacefully, control the lower classes, and keep them in their place so they don't interfere with elite goals.

Does this sound familiar? Like what has happened during the pandemic and in recent elections? Take a hard look at what has been done since the Presidency switched from Trump to Biden. There is no difference between Trump and Biden at all in policy, just in rhetoric and posturing. Same COVID plan. Same economic plans. Same social plans. Nothing changes when parties change power, and never has for well over a century.

Like when Democrat Grover Cleveland got elected in 1884, he assured corporations and the rich, just like Biden did, that nothing would fundamentally change for them with the transfer of power.

"No harm shall come to any business interest as the result of administrative policy so long as I am president…a transfer of executive control from one party to another does not mean any serious disturbance of existing conditions."

And here is a quote from Joe Biden to his wealthy donors from 2019, when running against Donald Trump. Sound similar?

"(If I get elected) No one's standard of living will change, nothing would fundamentally change."

Are you wondering how we will make any change in our country with this belief system of our ruling elite and their henchmen? Our government, by definition, opposes any change to the current social contract between the rich and everyone else and will work to stop it with all means at its disposal. Just like they violently and mercilessly shut down Occupy Wall Street and Black Lives Matter protests with their vicious police goon squads.

The focus of our elections on superficial and trite issues was established way back then, too—no honest discussion of problems, and no clear plan on what would get done moving forward. What you now see in personality politics started then, as to whether you liked a candidate, who they were having sex with, and other trivial issues.

A quote from Henry Adams, a commentator at the time –

"Very great issues are involved, but no one talks about real interests. By common consent, they agree to let these alone. We are afraid to discuss them. Instead of this, the press is engaged in a most amusing dispute whether Mr. Cleveland had an illegitimate child and did or did not live with more than one mistress."

What I am trying to show and explain to everyone is that America is the way it is today **by design**. There was an unofficial socio-economic system set up in the 19th century that had no relation to democracy or what people think America is all about.

The real America has a one-party system, not two. In it are two groups, in fact, factions of the same party: a pro-business party that gives endless money and subsidies to large businesses and wealthy individuals for free. In this system, small businesses and individual citizens are allowed to starve and die since they don't deserve hand-outs, unlike our great financial and corporate leaders, who deserve the money and will do something great with it (like give it to themselves for another mega yacht).

For example, in the early 20th century, President Grover Cleveland vetoed a bill to give $100,000 to farmers for seed grain during a drought, saying giving them aid would *'weaken their character.'* But around the same time, he gave $45 million in profit to bondholders by paying them above-market rates, just as a little thank-you to the investor class. Notice how giving people who own bonds free money is not hurting their character, but giving farmers money for grain to eat is somehow detrimental to them.

It was around this time that Congress established a national bank, effectively putting the government into a true partnership with private banking interests, guaranteeing their profits. As things grew more profitable for the ruling class and elite due to advances in technology and production techniques, they grew worse and worse for the working class. In 1864, in response to numerous national and local strikes over poor working conditions and wages, the U.S. government enacted the Contract Labor Law. This law allowed companies to sign contracts with foreign workers to replace domestic workers with cheap, easy-to-exploit labor and strikebreakers.

Does this sound familiar, given what is going on today with globalization and the use of cheap overseas labor to replace domestic labor? With laws like NAFTA, and tactics like H1B visas being used to replace domestic technology workers with lower-paid Indian workers? They have just modernized this system of social repression, wage suppression, and worker silencing through modern laws and methods. The laws in the United States of America are created for one reason and one reason only – to maximize the transfer of wealth to the ruling class from other citizens lower on the social class pyramid.

Check out this quote from a Labor Party speaker in 1890. Doesn't this sound like something from the Occupy Wall Street movement just a few years ago? How have things changed in America in 130 years?

"Wall Street owns the country. It is no longer a government of the people, by the people, and for the people, but a government of Wall Street, by Wall Street, and for Wall Street."

EVEN when poor, abusive, and exploitative conditions led to public outrage and pressure for reforms, the very vehicle meant for holding power accountable was neutered and redirected from its inception. For example, in 1890, the Sherman Antitrust Act was passed. The act defined itself as "an act to protect trade and commerce against unlawful restraints" (e.g., monopolization). It made it illegal to form a conspiracy to restrain trade in interstate or foreign commerce (e.g., price fixing and collusion). Reforms like the Sherman Anti-Trust Act were quickly undermined and weaponized against the working class by the ruling elite's legal front organization, the Supreme Court.

The SCOTUS is yet another institution in the USA in which the appearance of fairness and indifference to class shields the organization's true intent. The reality of SCOTUS is that they are elitist representatives of the oligarchy, helping resolve conflicts between ruling-class factions and families. Chosen by the President and serving as lifetime appointees, Supreme Court members are almost exclusively wealthy lawyers and almost always come from the upper classes.

In 1895, the SCOTUS made the Sherman Act toothless by declaring that industry monopolies, like the sugar industry, were based in manufacturing, not commerce, and therefore not regulated by the Act (what?). The court also said the Sherman Act could be used to break worker strikes since by not working, they were impeding commerce (wait, didn't they say sugar was manufacturing, not commerce? So, how are the workers impeding commerce but their company is not?). The court repeatedly refused to enforce the Sherman Act as written, and regulatory agencies have repeatedly refused to implement it as written. The SCOTUS has repeatedly declined to break up the monopolies for which the law was created.

Another example of reforms gutted by the elitist SCOTUS is the 14th Amendment. The 14th Amendment was supposed to ensure freedom and protection for blacks from white abuse and bigotry post-slavery. Still, the law was in reality used as protection for corporations further to enslave all American workers, black and white.

IN 1893, there was yet another depression and financial panic, unavoidable in a system of unending capitalist growth and expansion. Boom-and-bust cycles were indicative of this economic outlook and philosophy, and kept recurring every few decades without fail. After the SCOTUS gutted the Sherman Act within 5 years of its inception to benefit monopolies and break worker strikes, it then went after the 14th Amendment, which was ratified in 1868 with the intent to protect the rights of native-born African Americans post-slavery. Quickly after the ratification of the amendment, the SCOTUS interpreted it in a way to benefit and protect corporations, not black citizens. This was deliberate and planned, not some weird legal nuance they always like to attribute to SCOTUS decisions. In America, for the past 150 years, laws intended and promoted for a specific objective have been repurposed and redirected from the outset by their lackeys in the courts to align with the goals and objectives of the elite rich.

In 1877, there was a critical case that seemed innocuous on the surface but had a profound effect on how the United States has grown and developed, and what our country has become versus what it may have been intended to be. A Supreme Court decision (Munn v. Illinois) was made in which it determined that a grain elevator company was, in fact, a person being deprived of their property right. The SCOTUS did this through a twisted interpretation of the 14th Amendment, a use never intended. The amendment says that "nor shall any state deprive any person of life, liberty, or property without due process of law." Initially, the SCOTUS ruled that grain elevators were not people, but within a year, the American Bar Association got the ruling overturned. The Supreme Court quickly agreed with the bar association and held that corporations are people with inherent rights protected by the 14th Amendment. That year, the Supreme Court struck down 230 state laws intended to regulate corporations.

The cover story is that the 14th Amendment was passed to protect the rights of African Americans. The reality is it was promoted that way for PR and used in a totally different way than intended from its inception. As evidence of this,

Between 1890 and 1910, only 19 of the 14th Amendment cases involved blacks, while 288 involved corporations.

The numbers don't lie; the 14th Amendment was twisted and changed almost the moment it was passed to benefit the rich and corporations by the supposedly independent and unbiased Supreme Court. Justice and integrity indeed.

To give you an idea of the elitism and condescension towards the middle and working class from the SCOTUS, even way back then, here is a quote from Justice David J. Brewer in 1893.

"It is the unvarying law that the wealth of the community will be in the hands of the few…The great majority of men are unwilling to endure that long self-denial and saving which makes accumulations possible…and hence it has always been, and until human nature is remodeled, always will be true, that the wealth of a nation is in the hands of the few, while the many subsist up the proceeds of their daily toil."

Notice there is no mention of inheritance. How most rich people inherit their money, not through denial or intense saving. The attitude and mindset of the SCOTUS are the same as those of many of our founding fathers a century earlier. The rich deserve to be where they are because they are more intelligent, more moral, and more ethical. And if you are poor, it's your fault because you are lazy, greedy, ignorant, and unsophisticated, and deserve everything you get. And those smart, rich people need to direct the rest of us since we are too stupid and irresponsible to direct ourselves.

IF you read the first book of this series, I discuss in detail how those in power control people to direct them where they want them to be, as well as support the rich's interests over your own self-interest. People in modern semi-open societies like ours need to be controlled by more than fear, violence, and law. They are more deftly controlled through indoctrination, conditioning, and programming before more aggressive methods are needed. Programmed into all Americans are base values and ideas that are now accepted truths. This programming comes from all sources: parents, schools, ads, and entertainment.

Here is the standard base programming put into every kid growing up in America: First, being rich means you are better than other people. You get where you are through hard work, ingenuity, and inherent talent, and poor people are where they deserve to be because they are lazy and not as smart or well-bred as you. But, if you are poor, you can pull yourself up by the bootstraps and become rich through hard work, religious and moral behavior, and cowtailing to the elites and the ruling class.

This was programmed and reinforced into the population by popular authors of the late 19th century, like Russell Conwell, who gave this speech called 'Acres of Diamonds' to 5,000 performances across the country, reaching millions of Americans.

"I say that you ought to get rich, and it is your duty to get rich...The men who get rich may be the most honest men in your community. Let me say this clearly…98% of the rich men in America are honest. That is why they are rich. I sympathize with the poor, but the number of poor who are to be sympathized with is very small. Let us remember there is not a poor person in the United States who was not made poor by his own shortcomings."

Does this statement ring true to you today? That all rich men are honest, and they got rich because of their sincere and upstanding character? That all the poor people in the USA are there because they deserve it? While this may be the current trope of the rich, it has no relation to reality and is completely unsubstantiated by data or historical precedent.

AFTER the immeasurable financial success of the American industrialists and bankers due to a resource-rich new country and increased worker productivity thanks to technological developments, these extremely wealthy individuals needed something to do with all their money, since buying their 6th mansion or 7th mega yacht loses some charm once you buy more than 5 of them. And the last thing these types of people want to do with their money is help out other people poorer than they are, since those poor people are shiftless and lazy and would only blow it on PlayStation games and weed.

To not only prop up their massive egos but to indoctrinate millions of people into their way of thinking (greedy and self-centered), all those rich guys went out and founded universities with their names on them. Those universities were created to produce the type of lackeys that robber barons wanted to run their companies, as well as to keep the worker rabble in line and under control.

Just as American public schools were initially developed to convert farm workers into factory workers and to prepare the poor and working class for what to expect in their social strata, more upper-level universities and elite institutions were created to indoctrinate and train people to be the overseers of the rank and file. These upper-crust people keep everyone in line by thinking what they are told to think and doing what they are told to do by their social betters.

One thing all public and private institutions teach in America, at all levels, is deference and submission to authority. This is core to the American psyche and belief system, and critical to keeping workers, soldiers, and citizens pointed in the right direction to benefit the ruling class, financially or otherwise. School curricula and textbooks were carefully censored to suppress dissent and questioning of authority. The educational programs themselves are made to increase obedience and reduce independent thought.

Here is a journalist from 1890 commenting on the atmosphere of public schools at the time. Does this sound like an educational system intended to educate citizens to participate in an open democracy? Or one designed to repress and control kids into being subservient and pliable?

"The unkindly spirit of the teacher is strikingly apparent; the pupils, being completely subjugated to her will, are silent and motionless, the spiritual atmosphere of the classroom is damp and chilly."

Keeping poor and working-class people uneducated and unable to create dissent was a deliberate policy in America in the mid-to-late 19th century. Here is a quote from the secretary of the Massachusetts Board of Education in 1859 to show what the intellectual liberal teacher class thought of ordinary workers –

"The owners of factories are more concerned than other classes regarding interest in the intelligence of their laborers. When the latter are well-educated and the former are disposed to deal justly, controversies and strikes can never occur, not can the minds of the masses be prejudiced by demagogues and controlled by temporary and factious considerations."

Further confirming this strategy to keep the working class uneducated and subservient to authority is Joel Sprint, in his book Education and the Rise of the Corporate State.

"The development of a factory-like system in the 19th-century schoolroom was not accidental."

Elite universities trained white-collar professionals who were expected to run things for the ruling class and to push the ruling class's ideology onto ordinary people. These middlemen, who included teachers, doctors, lawyers, engineers, and politicians, would be paid not only to keep the system going but also to serve as a buffer between the poor and working-class anger towards the ruling class.

REGARDLESS of all the indoctrination and programming, many Americans knew something was rotten in Denmark, and the bill of sale being sold to them about American equality and opportunity was not what the establishment claimed it was. Massive national protests and movements occurred in the 1880s and 1890s, larger than ever before in America, challenging the narrative that the world bankers and business leaders were manufacturing and enforcing through their ownership of private media.

As mentioned earlier, with business-friendly and anti-worker legislation, corporate leaders were able to bring in legions of immigrant laborers, who themselves were put into work caste systems where different nationalities brought varying wages and treatment. By 1880, 1/10 of California's entire population was Chinese immigrants. Seventy-five thousand were brought in to work dangerous railroad jobs for pennies. Chinese immigrants, like the Irish immigrants who came before them, were treated harshly with acts of extreme violence and lynching. For example, in Rock Springs, Wyoming, in 1885, white men attacked 500 Chinese miners, murdering 28 of them. Have you ever heard of this event before in history class? Isn't it interesting how events like this are erased from official historical accounts?

New immigrants were brought over in the thousands by unscrupulous contractors and were typically lied to about the work they would do and where they would go to do it. Many immigrant workers, women and children included, were forced to work at gunpoint, and given starvation wages and little food. This influx of foreign workers, as it does today, helped keep wages low for domestic workers and reduce the effectiveness of strikes. This is the American tradition of misdirection, in which immigrants are blamed and vilified for poor wages and a lack of jobs. The reality is that it's not the immigrants who are causing this situation. Still, the corporate leaders and government are deliberately manufacturing the situation for their benefit, at the expense of domestic American workers.

Immigrants, just like today's immigrant workers in corporations, were easier to control and generally more helpless than native US workers. Immigrant workers rarely spoke English, were displaced from familiar surroundings, and were easier to manipulate and pay low wages. Even better for elite corporate owners was the fact that there were limited labor laws, and they could force children and immigrants to work as well. In 1880, 1 out of 6 children under 16 was working 12-hour days, 7 days a week, in the USA. Women immigrants had very few rights and even fewer options to be able to survive. They could become servants (white slaves), factory workers in a clothing factory, or prostitutes if they were fortunate. Land of opportunity indeed.

For the next two decades, massive national protests and national worker movements did have some impact on the rights and treatment of US workers. It was in 1886 that the movement for an 8-hour workday gained steam. Three hundred fifty thousand workers across all industries and across the entire country went on strike. The elite (business and state) reaction to the protests was, as usual, violent, and the protesters responded in kind. The government, then, just like today, would use the violence associated with these protests as a rationale to repress and attack labor causes and their people. Hmm, sounds like anything going on with BLM, the police, and the state's reaction to it?

One final tool the corporations and government of the 19th century had, in the South at least, was prison slave labor, something that has come back in vogue in the USA recently. In the South, prisoners were typically leased to corporations as slave labor, further helping to keep wages down and break strikes.

I mention much of this non-financial information to show how intertwined money and social issues are in the USA. The money side is kept hidden and opaque from public view, buried under a shield of legal mumbo jumbo, privacy, and classified documents—all to provide the appearance of fairness and justice to the everyday citizen while fleecing them for wealth.

BY 1892, US workers were so unhappy and abused by the rich that they were striking all over the country for better wages, shorter hours, and safer conditions. Cities like New Orleans were shut down for days as half the city workers went on a general strike. Coal miners, railroad workers, steel workers, and copper miners were all having massive protests and strikes. Almost every strike was broken with guns and violence, by the local and state police, private investigator goons (Pinkertons) hired by corporations, or National Guard troops brought in by Governors.

In 1893, the U.S. financial system collapsed yet again due to uncontrolled growth, uncontrolled speculation, economic manipulation, and profiteering by the wealthy elite. In fact, pretty much every single financial collapse in the history of the U.S. is from these causes, which are fundamental to our system by design, not a side-effect. Uncontrolled growth and market 'corrections' (crashes) are what define capitalism as an economic system.

In 1893, due to the crash, 642 banks and 16,000 businesses failed. 20% of the population was unemployed, and there was no relief offered by the government to the people for this reckless speculation and market manipulation by the elite. This economic situation only deepened public discontent and sparked strikes, the largest of which was the railroad workers' strike of 1894. It took 14,000 police, militia, and federal troops to violently put down the strike in Chicago, leaving 34 strikers dead. This reminds me a bit of the 2008 financial crash and Great Recession. Not one financial criminal who crashed our economy was held accountable, and it was Obama who let them all walk scot-free.

While farmers had always had a tenuous hold on wealth due to Mother Nature and crop cycles, their financial pressures increased significantly when advances in industrialization, technology, and production processes forced them to take bank loans to pay for new equipment. Farmers also had to pay railroad companies for transportation of their harvests, as well as grain merchants and storage elevators. This system worked OK for farmers as long as prices were high, but when they went down, the services they depended on instead increased in price. The problem for farmers was that they could not control the cost of their own harvest, which fluctuated with market conditions. But the bankers, railroad owners, and merchants could charge whatever they wanted and raise prices when farmers were hurting the most. When a farmer couldn't pay rising prices, he had his home and land taken away, and soon became a renter on the land they used to own.

Does this sound familiar to today? People are not being able to afford to keep their homes after they went underwater in their mortgages during the 2008 crash, and now have to rent where they used to be able to buy, as hedge funds and corporations like Zillow buy up all the homes in cash offers over asking that ordinary people can't compete with.

FARMERS GET THE SHAFT

BY 1880, 25% of all farms were now rented by tenants, and many of those old owners who couldn't make their rent payments were further reduced to laborers on their own farms. Talk about degrading. This was the standard process used by the elite to steal land and homes from the ordinary citizen and give it to the rich through their corporations. Using debt as a way to enslave people has been done for thousands of years in all sorts of cultures, but in America, it has become an art form.

There were a few other key developments that illustrate how the government manipulated financial policy to benefit corporations and harm farmers and individual citizens. One way was for the government to keep the amount of money in circulation steady so that, as the population grew, there would be less and less money in circulation. Farmers had to pay off their debts with that money, which was getting harder to get due to a lack of supply since the government would not print more. But for bankers, this was a windfall. Since they were the ones loaning out money in limited circulation, when it was repaid, it was worth more because there was less of it. Do you get this grift? The Govt reduces the money supply, so bankers make more on loans and also screw over working-class people like farmers who can't keep up with spiraling debt, then foreclose on them. What do you think of the land of opportunity now? Maybe for banks and their elite owners, it is.

Another nice trick was a crop lien system that was initiated in the South, which kept farmers in a form of economic slavery while redistributing their money to the rich. For example, a farmer would go to a merchant to get supplies. Since farmers had to wait until their harvest came in to pay the merchant, the merchant took a lien on their harvest, which could carry an interest rate of up to 25% annually. Each year, the farmer's debt inevitably increased as he paid interest until he could pay it off; finally, his farm would be lost, and he would become a tenant on the land he used to own. Rinse and repeat for thousands of people.

BY the early 1900s, companies began to figure out how to deskill jobs so they could treat people as interchangeable components, making it easier to pay them lower wages and to fire and replace them. A new method called Taylorism was developed, which created a division of labor, increased mechanization, and introduced piecework wage systems. The goal was to give management control of every detail of a worker's time and energy in a factory. Does this sound like an Amazon warehouse today? Human workers became nothing more than standardized parts that could be bought and sold, and disposed of, as commodities. And without any substantive labor laws, immigrants of all ages were put to work for starvation wages in sweatshops. This is a quote from Edwin Markham in Cosmopolitan magazine in January 1907.

"In unaired rooms, mothers and fathers sew by day and night. The children are called in from play to work beside their elders. Nearly any hour on the East side of New York City, you can see them, pallid boy or spindling girl, their faces dulled, their backs bent under a heavy load of garment piled on head and shoulders..."

Workers in garment factories worked in draconian conditions, without drinking water, with floors covered in mice and roaches, with no heat in winter and no air in summer. A place where children worked with their parents 70-80 hours per week, 7 days a week.

This is how the ultra-rich in America have looted the country, beyond raping the environment. They bleed the working class and poor dry by working them to death for peanuts, by working poor children to death in their factories. These are the men who built America. This is how they made their fortunes.

For example, in 1911, a shirt factory caught on fire. The company kept the doors locked to keep its employees confined during working hours. People could not get out because the doors were locked. In the end, 146 workers, primarily women, were burned or crushed to death. One hundred thousand people marched in response.

In 1904, 27,000 workers were killed on the job. Accidents topped 50,000 in a year. In 1914, 35,000 workers were killed in industrial accidents, and 700,000 were injured.

Want an idea of how horrible it really was for children and other young people working under these barbaric conditions? This is a quote from a physician at the time –

"A considerable number of boys and girls die within the first two or three years after beginning work…36 out of 100 of all the men and women who work in the mill die before, or by the time they are 25 years of age."

Wondering what it was really like to work in a steel factory back then? In 1892, the Carnegie Steel plant in Pennsylvania had a 12-foot-high 3-mile fence around it, topped with barbed wire and gun holes. Does that sound like a private business or a prison with forced labor?

Here we see how far the ultra-rich go to take wealth from the lower and working classes. They cheat them in wages, work them to death, work children to death, and violently attack them for asking for better treatment. The government and police are there to protect and support the companies, not the citizens being abused. That is the role of the US government, as a business enabler and repressor of the working classes in support of the ruling class. The law, the military, and the police are in place to protect and support the rich, not the general populace.

THE *Deconstructing America* series is focused on exposing the true America behind the myths, propaganda, and historical narratives that have been accepted as truth through decades of indoctrination and conditioning. By providing you with information that the people currently in charge have decided not to share, I hope you will be better equipped to make authentic, independent decisions on your own, with as little outside influence as possible.

We began our journey by discussing how the Civil War marked a massive shift in control and ownership of the new nation, as Northern elites took power from Southern plantation owners to establish what we now know as the United States of America. The Civil War reshaped America, but not in the ways most people think. It enabled oligarchs (industrialists and affluent families), working through their flunkies in the government and the Supreme Court, to set up a game of loaded dice that has the appearance of fairness and justice but is in fact a system of exploitation and abuse.

During the Civil War, the government could force people to work at gunpoint, and elites could gouge consumers with high prices with no regulations, in which the ruling class took all the profits and gave nothing back to the workers. Rich people liked this situation and wanted to keep it going post-war in an unofficial shadow partnership between the police, state, and feds to keep the lower classes in line and exploitable for endless resources. As I mentioned before, the financial strategy of the elite in the United States of America has always been to use economic hardship and national disasters as opportunities to rob and exploit the working and middle classes and transfer wealth upwards in spurts.

Back in the 19th century, most of the modern methods for exploiting the general population for the benefit of the rich were established and are still used today. This is exemplified by the coronavirus pandemic, in which we saw the government focused on enabling profiteering by large companies at the expense of public health. At the same time, corporations gouged consumers and made massive profits while giving nothing back to their workers. We detailed many of these methods, including passing laws that sound like they will be used for the common good, when in fact, nuanced legal language is deliberately written to be misinterpreted by legal compatriots from the start. The corporate lawyers and the Supreme Court can come in and interpret those laws in ways that benefit the rich at the expense of everyone else.

The government, working in allegiance and deference to the elite oligarchy, used the law of eminent domain to legally steal land from hard-working farmers and homesteaders to give it to railroad companies and other large corporations. Modern legal concepts like *let the buyer beware* paved the way for predatory capitalism in America, giving corporations the legal right to cheat and lie to customers. By the late 19th century, America's entire legal system had been restructured to tilt the scales in favor of the elite at the expense of ordinary citizens, creating a legal framework that redistributed wealth upward from the most vulnerable sections of our society. Pull yourselves up by the bootstraps indeed.

Constant cyclical market panics and crashes every 10-15 years or so were an unavoidable result of the economic system of capitalism, which the United States more or less embraced from its inception. Still, it evolved into a whole new level by the late 19th century. These market crashes were met with massive strikes and protests, as the rich made out like bandits in good and bad times, while the ordinary citizen suffered and got next to nothing, no matter which way the wind was blowing. Strikes and protests were violently put down by the oligarchy's henchmen, including the legal system, police, National Guard troops, and private investigators, as well as immigrant workers who were used to lower wages and break strikes.

The myth of rags-to-riches and American exceptionalism was, and still is, an effective propaganda tool to keep regular people always reaching for a gold ring that is forever out of reach. This merging of historical fact and narrative fiction, as a way to profit from and manipulate the lower classes into specific behaviors, was established in the 19th century in America and has helped reinforce American values that benefit the ultra-rich at the working man's expense. The great American writers of the 19th century, along with some not-so-great ones, really constructed the fictionalized narrative that is now considered U.S. history. From romanticized tales about Christopher Columbus to stories of poor boys making it big through the generosity of the noble and moral rich, most of the American biases we see today are rooted in this period.

Because of the US government's lack of centralized planning, bankers like J.P. Morgan were able to create and maintain monopolies that eliminated fair competition in the marketplace. Businessmen were able to take advantage of their power and influence to make millions by eliminating competition, keeping prices high, keeping wages low through immigrant labor, and getting government subsidies for free land and money.

The U.S. government pretends to be neutral in all these affairs between different strata of society. Still, its true purpose is to settle upper-class disputes peacefully and keep the lower classes in line so they don't interfere with elite goals and profitability.

All the success of the Robber Barons led to the rest of America experiencing more abuse, poor wages, longer hours, and more injuries and deaths. The increasingly poor conditions were met with protests on a scale never seen before or since in America. Millions protested, went on strike, and brought national work and commerce to a halt. This was met first with violence by the oligarchy, and when they were unable to put down the protests by force, it was followed by the pretense of reforms from the ruling class and government. But just like with subsidies and other sleight-of-hand legislation, the reforms were made not just toothless from the start but were grossly misinterpreted to benefit the rich at everyone else's expense by the elitist Supreme Court.

In reality, the objective of the ruling class in granting concessions to workers back then (and now) was not to achieve class equality, but to keep the masses quiet and create a buffer of middle-class workers between the ruling class and the working class. These middle-class buffers, who became our modern businessmen and professionals, help cushion class anger from below as well as keep those below them economically in line. The workers and poor below the middle-class workers, both white and black, saw little change to their material conditions and daily life regardless of who was in power and what novel reforms were made.

The next significant step in our nation's transformation into a shadow corporate state was when an obscure 1877 trial involving a grain elevator company led the Supreme Court to twist the 14th Amendment, declaring that corporations were, in fact, people, with all the rights inherent in that status. Now corporations can own things and buy and sell things, but cannot be held accountable for their actions like a person can. Convenient for those business owners, huh? They commit horrific crimes against humanity, and their company, not them, gets a fine. All by design.

The growth of U.S. industries and their profitability were driven by several deliberate government and corporatist efforts. First, the government set high tariffs for foreign goods to keep out foreign steel and materials to benefit U.S. oligarchs; second was industrialists eliminating competition through monopolies and keeping prices high through price-fixing; third the government giving private businesses free land and money with no strings; and fourth by working hundreds of thousands of men, women and children 12+ hours per day, 7 days per week for near-starvation wages.

Another clever method the establishment has for making us think we are making progress, while the rich, in turn, loot programs, is the Interstate Commerce Act of 1887. This act, like many others, has regulations that are both nominal and optional, so it's up to companies to decide whether to meet them. What this does is provide the illusion of regulation to the general public while, in fact, giving away the farm to private business interests.

Americans are indoctrinated and conditioned from youth to not only accept this abusive and exploitative system but to champion it and die on the hill for it if necessary. They will defend the elite's right to take whatever they want, however they want, because it is core to their belief system to submit to authority blindly.

Everything in America has been built and constructed to achieve the dual goal of enabling elite profitability and lower-class repression. The educational system is designed to manufacture obedient laborers and office workers who do what they are told, do not question or even know how to reason, and help to create a nice buffer between millions of angry poor and working-class people and the ultra-rich. Immigrants are shipped in by the million for cheap and exploitable labor to take work from domestic workers and keep wages and strikes down.

From the very beginning, from the Revolutionary War days on, the American elites who manufactured the revolution to take power from British elites pitted the poor against each other. They pitted slaves and poor whites against each other, all to misdirect class anger away from themselves and keep the people fighting and distracted. This has worked like a charm for hundreds of years to keep people in line with minimal violence, at least since the 19th century.

I leave you with this quote from SCOTUS Justice Louis Brandeis in his book *Other People's Money*.

"They control people through the people's own money."

This is the great secret in the United States regarding power and control. This is how the ordinary citizen is controlled beyond all the programming and threats of fear and intimidation. Your own money, or lack thereof, is what enslaves you. You, as a citizen, in the eyes of the ruling elite class, are nothing more than a disposable commodity to be exploited for as much profit as possible, at any cost to your health or well-being.

This is a pamphlet of common sense, and it is addressed to the inhabitants of America, every single one of them.